To Date
or
Not to Date

What the Bible Says about
Premarital Relationships

D. Kevin Brown

Energion Publications
Gonzalez, FL
2014

ISBN10: 1-63199-003-9
ISBN13: 978-1-63199-003-8

Energion Publications
P. O. Box 841
Gonzalez, FL 32560

energion.com
pubs@energion.com
850-525-3916

PREFACE

Dating has become a totally accepted practice in America and even in the Church. Yet what I hope to show in this book is the fact that dating (as we know it today), does not appear in the pages of the Bible. It's my desire to awaken within the hearts and minds of parents and young people alike the understanding that we can trust the Bible to guide us in all things, including premarital relationships. My prayer is you will be inspired to go against the grain of the culture and follow the timeless truths of Scripture and seek the best God has for you in all things.

Please know this book will go counter to almost everything you and I know about relationships and thus it will challenge on many levels. I am not naive. I recognize this book is not likely to change the tide of our culture or society, but it is my deep desire to raise the bar in our thinking concerning God's ways in seeking a future mate. Therefore, I dedicate this book to all those who will choose the way less traveled. I'm excited to know you desire to experience the blessing of allowing the Word of God to be a lamp unto your feet and a light unto your path.

A huge thank you to my wife, Pam! Thanks for reading and re-reading this book and helping me to see things from a "lady's perspective." You are amazing! Lastly, a big "thank you" goes to Henry Neufeld for publishing this book and being such an enormous blessing to me! Thanks Henry for touching so many lives through Energion Publications!

PROBLEM ON AISLE 9

Bill and his wife Phyllis, along with their three children make the turn at aisle 9 in the local grocery store. Two loaves of bread are on the list and this is the aisle. All is well until Bill bumps into a lady who promptly says, "Well hi, Billy! It's been forever since I've seen you! I just moved back to town last week!"

Bill is now three shades of bright red, and sheepishly says, "Hi Susie, nice to see you."

Little Bobby asks, "Who dat daddy? Who dat?"

Bill squirms. He never looks directly at his three-year-old son. "Uh, well, uh ..."

Susie enthusiastically responds as she kneels down to rub Bobby's head, "Well Bobby, I was your daddy's girlfriend! He took me to the prom two years in a row. Well, that is after he dumped his 10th grade girlfriend. What was her name Billy?"

"Uh ... oh ... ah ... that doesn't really matter now," says Bill. 'Uh ... Susie Epperson, this is my son Bobby. He just turned three and these are my two daughters, Megan, who is eight and our oldest, Mary Anna. She's ten." Bill now looking at his wife says, "I believe you know Susie, don't you, honey?"

Phyllis, with a look of resignation says, "Yes Bill. I know Susie."

Just how many times this embarrassing scenario plays out, no one could possibly know. But, one thing is for sure, a past relationship being brought to light is never fun or easy to explain. And contrary to Bill's statement to his young son, "... that doesn't really matter now," well, that's not really true. It does matter. It matters a lot! Can you imagine how awkward it will be for Bill to see Susie four more times on every aisle before he and his family can finally get out of the store? Excruciating!

Think about the conversations which will continue in the car on the way home? What does Bill say to his two girls? Does he want this scenario to play out for them one day down the road in their lives? I hope not! But the truth is, according to our cultural norms, this will likely be the case. It doesn't have to be! We don't have to live a life littered with relationship regrets. There is a better way. In fact there is a much better way. There are patterns and principles found in the pages of the Bible providing a path to a vision which can eliminate the opportunity for any awkward and embarrassing moments in a grocery store aisle.

GOING FOR GOLD

What medal do Olympic athletes shoot for when they go to the Olympics? Bronze? Silver? I don't think so. They go for the gold! Why would you train and sacrifice so much and not go for the best? Go for gold! That's my desire in this book. I want to inspire you to go for the best! I want to inspire you to go for the gold!

What if you could arrive on your wedding day and marry your spouse with no baggage of past relationships in tow? What if you never had to bring up the "other ones" in any conversation with your spouse? What if there weren't any "other ones" at all? I can speak from experience here. I wish with all of my heart that what I just described to you could have been the case in my life on December 22, 1990, the day I married my wife. Yet it was most definitely not the case for me or her.

I can honestly say that I was only doing what everyone else was doing and I didn't know any better. I didn't know that I could even go for gold! I didn't know that I was supposed to even try. The problem with dating in our culture is that for most, there is no understanding of what we're really to be shooting for in terms of our future and relationships. We're not training for anything, much less a gold medal. Thus, dating is most often a pointless, purposeless, and intentionless endeavor. It's just something you do as a pre-teen and teen because everyone else is doing it. There is no purpose or vision in that. It's like having the ability to win a gold medal and you don't even try.

Ask yourself this question: Where does dating lead for many teens? You won't have to think long to answer, because we all know where it most often leads: sexual promiscuity, lost innocence, emotional heartache and aisle 9 awkwardness for the future. Truth is, dating has become a practice for divorce. After all, just because you slide a ring on someone's finger at a wedding someday doesn't mean you are going to stop what you've been practicing for 10 years in the turnstile of swapping off partners in multiple relationships. And that's the undeniable mark of dating in our culture. The high divorce rate in our nation confirms this premise.

It's time we raise the bar! It's time to want better for our young people than the purposeless, casual, intentionless relationships we've become satisfied with over the last several decades. Let's go for gold!

A Better Way?

I will tell you now as I study the pages of Scripture, I do not see a cookie cutter, specific "cut and dried" formula for how one might arrive to the wedding altar. I can't point to chapter and verse in the Bible and say, "Look! There it is! That's how it's done." Truth is there are no two examples in Scripture that are exactly alike regarding relationships. Yet, there are principles and patterns in Scripture that give us very good direction and guidance on how we might choose to live.

Just as there is not a "sinner's prayer" per se in Scripture that one might point to and say, "Pray this exact prayer to become a born again, believer in Christ," I'm also keenly aware there is not a formulaic A, B, C, D pattern we may follow, like baking a cake, to explain all the nuances of premarital relationships. Yes, regarding salvation, we know we must pray, confess and repent of our sins and "call on the name of the Lord" to become a believing follower of Jesus Christ. But even that experience was different for the Ethiopian Eunuch, the Philippian jailer, Lydia the seller of purple, Cornelius the centurion and Nicodemus the Pharisee. Yet there are guiding principles in the pages of Scripture to serve as a lamp to our feet and a light to our path (Psalm 119:105).

ASSUMPTIONS

May I make some assumptions? Yes, I know it's dangerous to assume anything, but for the sake of argument, I'm going to assume if you are reading this book you might be a parent, grandparent or young adult (teenager) who is looking for a better way for your children, grandchildren, or for yourself. I will also assume if you are married, it's likely you are not married to the "one and only" person you ever dated. However, I will assume if you could go back and do it over again, you would. And, if you could do it all over again, I'm going to assume you would only date your current spouse. (If this is not the case, then something might be wrong in your spirit and heart.)

As parents, I believe we desire something better for our sons and daughters. As a young adult, you probably want more for yourself than just being a part of the meat market of dating. Therefore, with those assumptions in play, I want to share with you a grander vision of something far better than that which we've all been swallowing for the last 50-60 years in our western culture. I believe you desire a greater vision than the current dating merry-go-round of purposeless relationships that often lead to broken hearts, emotional turmoil and a much greater likelihood for future divorce after marriage.

You see, I wish someone had told me what I'm going to share with you when I was young. I have the relationship baggage just like our fictional character, Bill, on aisle 9 of the grocery. Most likely, if you are a married adult reading this book, you do too. Why? Because you and I were simply following the accepted patterns and cultural norms of our society. Everyone dated. It's what we did. We started out as little kids by passing notes in third grade that said, "Check 'yes' if you like me and 'no' if you don't." We've all been conditioned to date people in order to find "Mr. or Mrs. Right." Even as Christians, we are following the exact same patterns of this world. We're no different. The Bible says in Romans 13:12-14:

The night is far gone; the day is at hand. So then let us cast off the works of darkness and put on the armor of light. Let us walk properly as in the daytime, not in orgies and drunkenness, not in sexual immorality and sensuality, not in quarreling and jealousy. But put on the Lord Jesus Christ, and make no provision for the flesh, to gratify its desires.

WHAT DO YOU BELIEVE ABOUT THE BIBLE?

In the last paragraph, I quoted the Apostle Paul's admonition to the Romans from the Bible. I'm quoting Scripture because I'm convinced it is the sole authority for all of life. As I stated at the beginning of this book, I'm assuming you are likely a professing Christian. I might be wrong and if I am, I pray you would trust Jesus Christ as your Lord and Savior. But, assuming I'm right, I'm also going to assume that you believe the Bible is the "word" of the living God.

But what I don't want to assume is what you believe about the Bible and it's authority over your life. I know you're probably okay with saying the Bible is the "Word of God," but to what degree do you believe the Bible is authoritative and sufficient to guide your life and mine as our moral compass? The reason I bring this up is because from this point forward I'm going to use the Bible as the sole guide for framing our discussions about relationships. After all, the subtitle of this book is: What the Bible Says about Premarital Relationships. I'm going to ask you to clear everything else from your mind and let's use nothing but the Bible to shape and form our thinking.

This sounds fairly simple, but I assure you it's not. We all have a grid and a way of thinking that has been shaped by our childhood experiences, our educational experiences, our entertainment choices, etc. So, while we might think that we are making decisions based upon the tenets and principles outlined in Scripture, we might not be. In order to think biblically, we must kick out of our brains what popular culture says and thinks about relationships. What I will share with you in this book will not be politically correct. So for now, please try to push out of your head what the talk show hosts and social gurus of our day say about relationships.

I am a "Biblicist." What is that? I believe the Bible is literally God's word to us. I believe 2 Timothy 3:16-17 wholeheartedly:

> All Scripture is breathed out by God and profitable for teaching, for reproof, for correction, and for training in righteousness, that the man of God may be complete, equipped for every good work.

The Bible is a supernatural book and is sacred and literally breathed out by God. The apostle Peter said much the same thing in 1 Peter 1:19-21:

> And we have the prophetic word more fully confirmed, to which you will do well to pay attention as to a lamp shining in a dark place, until the day dawns and the morning star rises in your hearts, knowing this first of all, that no prophecy of Scripture comes from someone's own interpretation. For no prophecy was ever produced by the will of man, but men spoke from God as they were carried along by the Holy Spirit.

I'm seeking to build on the solid rock foundation of God's word, not on man's ways, not on what's culturally acceptable or politically correct. But I know the arguments and I know what some of you might be thinking. You might be contemplating, "Well, the Bible was written a long time ago and while I believe it's the Word of God, I'm not sure it's applicable for today." My response: Are we to be pitied because we weren't born in Bible times? God intended for His Word to be applicable for all generations.

I believe God was smart enough and wise enough to divinely inspire the 40 authors of His Word to write in such a way that what was written in the first century and beyond to be applicable in the 21st century as well. God is not dumb. He stands outside of time. He is the Alpha and the Omega, the Beginning and the End. He knows your next thought before you think it. He sees tomorrow before it happens. He's the same, yesterday, today and forever. No, the Bible is not bound in time. It's timeless! It will shape and form our thinking if we'll let it. Thus, the Bible and its principles will be the framework we use going forward in this book.

So How Did We Get Here?

Before WWII the current concept and idea of dating didn't exist. Prior to the 1940's, people "courted," which is really a watered-down form of betrothal, which we will discuss in detail a bit later. The divorce rate prior to WWII was extremely low (almost non-existent). Being divorced carried with it a heavy social stigma. But something happened. After WWII, America became a very prosperous nation and we slowly but surely began a steady march away from the Lord and Biblical principles. This decline continues almost unabated in our country. As the children of Israel did in Scripture, we have forgotten the Lord (Deut. 7:10-15). In the 1950's we entered the era of "Happy Days." Parents started providing their teens the keys to the car and off to the drive-in they went. Dating was born.

The dating relationships I had and those I continue to observe today are by and large casual in nature and done mostly to get to know someone or just to have fun. I think any honest observer of "dating" today would probably agree it is seldom done with any intentionality or purpose.

I know there are many ways to define dating. But for the purpose of this book, I'm going to use the definition of dating as this: a casual relationship with little or no intentionality other than to have a good time and to get to know a person. I could even describe it as recreational romance.

I know many people who say they are dating with purpose and they are "committed" to the other person. Okay, great! My concern is at what point does that commitment stop? Is it when you have an argument? Is it when you don't make each other happy anymore or someone new and better comes along? You see, that's a recipe for

8

future divorce and you are practicing how to do it now. I often tell young people: **Please don't deceive yourself into thinking you are dating with purpose and commitment if that purpose and commitment can be tossed away at a moment's notice. That's not true commitment, that's selfishness.**

THE CONSEQUENCES

So what are the consequences of dating? What has dating done to our society? It's helped to decimate the family. We have a divorce rate in this nation of over 50% and young people are going through multiple relationships like a turnstile at a stadium. Thus we have a soiled morality, broken hearts, and devastated children. Many Christians have assumed it is normal and healthy for young people to experience several dating relationships prior to selecting a spouse. For whatever reason, these recreational romances are assumed and considered to be some sort of emotional preparation for marriage. But dating is not natural. It's artificial. It's play acting. When a person goes on a date, they are showing their best to that other person. It's not real life. We dress up and spruce up and put our best foot forward and off we go to dinner and a movie. That is an artificial environment and certainly not an ideal situation.

These *temporary* and often fake romantic relationships are not God's ideal. Surely God does not desire for young couples to become romantically involved with one another when they are 12 and 13 years old. Is partner-swapping for ten to fifteen years, from a person's mid-teens to their late 20's, and then finally marriage, God's design? It cannot be healthy for young people to "practice" divorce for 10-15 years. My former basketball coach always said, "You play like you practice!" Amen, Coach!

Dating today often teaches that it is okay to break up at any time for any reason. You can even do it via a text message or via social media. No problem! Yet, in breaking up, these two hearts, (which have likely begun to bond emotionally) will be ripped apart. They leave each other with at least some degree of heart-break. And they will likely leave with varying degrees of emotional wounding and scarring. But soon the pain of breaking up is pushed to the back of their brain, numbed perhaps, and before long there is a new romance with a different partner. Yet even young wounds leave deep scars and over a period of several years of experiencing these emotional break-ups has a cumulative effect on a person's heart. It becomes increasingly calloused and unable to love deeply and commit wholeheartedly.

Finally the young person "finds" the one they will eventually marry. (I place the word "finds" in quotations because it doesn't have to be this way. It's God sovereignty that brings a person into a believer's life. Will we trust Him?) But the memories of past romances, the pattern of broken relationships without question will indelibly mark the brain and the heart forever.

NOT STICKY

Have you ever tried to use a sticky note which would no longer stick? Maybe you used it as a bookmark or on your refrigerator, but it no longer sticks. That's frustrating. We all know the "sticky" will eventually wear off of an overused sticky note. This analogy works for relationships too.

As a young couple becomes romantically involved with one another, they begin to bond emotionally. They increasingly share their hearts with one another. Their thoughts and imaginations are focused on their partner. What they have done is to begin the God-designed process of becoming "one," even if there is virtually no physical relationship. They become one heart long before they become "one flesh." It's like taking both your hands and putting them together with all your fingers touching. Yet, we tell our young people it is okay to date and get to know the opposite sex, but don't have sex. That's like putting both hands together with all fingers touching except the two ring fingers. Eventually they'll touch (representing what's to be done only in marriage … sex).

Neuroscientists tell us sexual activity releases brain chemicals which trigger emotional bonding and a powerful desire to repeat the activity. Breaking these bonds over and over makes it much harder later in life to bond with a future spouse.

As I worked my way through writing this book, it galvanized in my own heart once again the very idea of recreational romance has created a revolving door mentality for our young people. They have been exposed to so many relationships prior to marriage, no wonder they find it so hard to eventually settle down with one spouse. They are simply repeating what they've been doing for years. When a minister asks a bride and groom to place rings on each other's fingers and repeat, "Till death do us part," it means almost nothing today. Do we really believe a ring on our left hand is going to change what's been trained in the brain?

We just talked about being "sticky" and Jesus spoke of this idea in Matthew 19:4-6.

> He answered, "Have you not read that he who created them from the beginning made them male and female, and said, 'Therefore a man shall leave his father and his mother and hold fast to his wife, and the two shall become one flesh'? So they are no longer two but one flesh. What therefore God has joined together, let not man separate."

Did you see those two words in verse 5, "hold fast?" Those words mean to "cleave" or "be glued to." But that's impossible if we've lost our sticky! Just how many times can a person be in a relationship and give his or her heart away to someone before he or she cannot stick anymore? This cleaving and uncleaving is not what God intended for us. It is not how God expects us to arrive to the marriage altar. But, then again, just what is marriage?

MARRIAGE: A PICTURE OF CHRIST AND THE CHURCH

Our society as a whole has become very flippant about marriage. Marriage has become somewhat of a joke in America. Many people are no longer getting married at all. Cohabitation is rampant and "no fault" divorces, where both parties can walk away, are chalked up as a mistake.

Marriage is critical to a stable society. Without it you eventually have chaos. If you don't believe that, just take a few minutes and read Romans chapter one, where homosexuality is addressed. Marriage is not to be between two men or two women. That's not God's divine design. Remember, Jesus said in Matthew 19 that a "**man** will leave his father and mother and cleave to his **wife**."

Cohabitation and homosexuality have been embraced in this country. Biblical marriage is on the decline. The nuclear family is disappearing in America and with that disappearance has come the appearance of homes without fathers and with massive poverty. You read any study you like on the socioeconomic impacts of homes without fathers and you'll see the devastating effects of a "marriage-less" America.

Think about what marriage represents in Scripture. Marriage is the representation of the Father, (God), offering to send his son, Jesus for the bride (the Church). God could have used any other analogy He wanted to describe the relationship between His Son and the Church, but He chose marriage. Paul said to the church at Corinth in 2 Corinthians 11:2-3:

> For I feel a divine jealousy for you, since I **betrothed you to one husband**, to present you as a pure virgin to Christ. But I am afraid that as the serpent deceived Eve by his cunning, your thoughts will be led astray from a sincere and pure devotion to Christ. (My emphasis added.)

Marriage symbolizes and signals to mankind the love the Father has for us, the Church. He wants to give the Church (that's us, as believers) to His Son (the Groom), clean and pure. There is 100% commitment here. Dating is the absolute antithesis of that picture. Jesus is not dating us. He paid a great price for the Church.

THE BRIDE'S PRICE AND BETROTHAL

Have you heard those terms: **bride's price** and **betrothal** before? Maybe you have, but you might struggle to define them. Honestly, I didn't fully understand these terms until I began to dig deeper into the Bible about premarital relationships. The terms **bride's price** and **betrothal** continually pop up either in name or in practice in the pages of Scripture.

Scripturally, in order for a young man to be qualified to call on or pursue a young lady, he must first be able to show to the father of the young lady that he is capable of paying the **bride's price** for her. In other words, he must show that he can make provision for her. Let's put it in our vernacular today. He's got to have a **job**! If he can't provide for her, then he cannot legitimately and biblically pursue her heart. However this process of pursuing her is one that is much deeper and much more committed than what we know of today. It's called: **betrothal**.

As I have studied Hebrew customs over the years (and I'm not a Hebrew scholar by any means), I have encountered a process that is almost totally unknown today. In the ancient Hebrew culture, a young man and a young lady would see each other in the community and they would become attracted to each other and they would discuss this attraction with their families (unlike today, where parents are simply "informed" as to whom their son or daughter is dating). The custom was for the fathers of both the young man and young lady to discuss together, as families, the relationship between their son and daughter. At that time, the prospective bride's father would ask the prospective groom's father about the bride's price. Only then would they become betrothed to one another. In other words, there was a commitment that was so binding only a certificate of divorce could break it.

In the gospels of Matthew and Luke we read that Mary was betrothed to Joseph. The Bible says in Matthew 1:18-19:

> Now the birth of Jesus Christ took place in this way. When his mother Mary had been **betrothed** to Joseph, before they came together she was found to be with child from the Holy Spirit. And her **husband** Joseph, being a just man and unwilling to put her to shame, resolved to **divorce** her quietly. (My emphasis added.)

Joseph is called "husband." Customarily during the betrothal, the young man and young lady were already being called "husband" and "wife." Until Joseph understood God's plan for the virgin birth, he could only assume Mary had been with another man. So, he planned to divorce her quietly. Again, a certificate of divorce was required to break the betrothal. It was only the act of consummation (sexual intercourse) which sealed the marriage.

Jesus would grow up and ultimately give us the greatest example in all Scripture of the payment of the bride's price. He willingly paid the bride's price to the Father (God) for His bride. 1 Corinthians 6:19-20 tells us:

> Or do you not know that your body is a temple of the Holy Spirit within you, whom you have from God? You are not your own, for you were **bought with a price**. So glorify God in your body. (My emphasis added.)

Think about the fact that Jesus is betrothed to the Church right now. Ultimately, He came from His Father's house to where we live, earth. He showed the Father He was willing to pay the bride's price for the bride (the Church) with his death on the cross. Now try to grasp this next thought: Jesus Christ died for the Church when He was **only betrothed** to her? Wow! Can you grasp the seriousness of betrothal?

I hope you are beginning to see some biblical parallels between what relationship-making should look like in our lives as modeled for us by God the Father and His Son (the groom) and the bride (the Church). Again, Jesus is not dating us. He is betrothed to us. He committed Himself to one bride and one bride only. God modeled this in the Garden of Eden, when He brought only one woman, Eve, to Adam. God didn't make 10 women and ask Adam to try them all out (date them) to see with whom he was most compatible and satisfied. That's a ludicrous thought. God designed Eve to be the perfect and suitable helper for Adam. Eve completed Adam and Adam completed Eve. God knew exactly what He was doing when in His sovereignty, He brought them together. You see, there are absolutely no biblical parallels to the idea of dating in Scripture. It simply doesn't exist. We can trust God to bring that perfect one to us, just as He did for Adam and Eve.

And just think … one day Jesus is coming back for the Church. Jesus said in John Chapter 14 He was going away to prepare a place for us and He's coming back to take us to be with Him. Right now He's gone away (as the Groom) and He is making provision for the bride, the Church. And once those provisions are made, He will return for the Church and there will be a wedding in heaven. Jesus will marry the Church and this wedding will be followed by a grand reception called "The Marriage Supper of the Lamb" (Rev. 19:6-9). I can't wait! That will be the wedding of all weddings and the reception of all receptions!

What about Falling in Love?

I can hear it now: "But what about love? Where is the opportunity for them to **fall in love**?" Another popular question might be, "When are young people supposed to begin to bond emotionally and see if they are compatible?" Those are legitimate questions, but they are not exactly the best or most biblical questions to ask. So, let me ask a question or two. Is falling in love like falling off the sofa during a nap? Is falling in love like having an accident, oops! Or could it be that we are somehow unknowingly or unwittingly bitten by a love bug or pierced by an arrow from Cupid's bow? Is that how love and relationships work? We just fall into them?

15

First of all, it's been said that when you **fall**, you most often don't know where you are going to land. So I don't like the idea of falling. Second, the whole "love-at-first-sight," mantra is often heralded as the "perfect way to fall in love." Yes, there might be physical attraction at first, but not committed, dedicated love. As human beings we are not to be ruled and governed by our emotions only. Emotions are fickle and can easily mislead us.

Think about this fact: **If you are a believer in Jesus Christ, haven't you chosen to love Him without seeing Him?** You have never seen Jesus and neither have I. Isn't it amazing that we have been betrothed to Jesus Christ, sight unseen? We chose to receive Him by faith and we have never seen Him! This fact reminds me of the account in Genesis 24 when Rebekah agreed to become Isaac's wife having never seen him before. That's trust! That's faith! That's true love!

Let's be reminded, God has a perfect design for all of our lives. If He is sovereign (and He is), then we can know without a doubt He's got a plan for whom we are to marry. Yet when I say this, I'm afraid some might think I'm advocating relationships where there is no love. Well, I'm not! I can assure you of that. But **falling in love** is simply not mentioned in the Bible. Men are simply told to love their wives and the wives are told to respect their husbands (Eph. 5:33).

Love is a **decision**. Love is so much more than feelings or butterflies in our stomachs. It's more accurate to say we **choose** to love. We choose to love even when the feelings aren't there. Why? Because our feelings will ebb and flow and come and go, but the decision to love doesn't waver. It's been said it's not **true love** until there is sacrifice. If you've been married for any length of time, you know this to be true. One of the reasons we have such a high divorce rate is because people decide to stop loving. They have not **fallen out of love**; they have simply decided to stop loving. They made the mental choice to stop loving and give up.

We are not to be led by our emotions. We are to be led by the will of God. Emotions are a wonderful gift from God, but they are not to lead us. Solomon told his son in Proverbs 23:19, "Hear, my son, and be wise, and direct your heart in the way."

We must "direct" our hearts. Love is to be based on our willingness to surrender to God's will. Romance will follow. We are all too often getting the cart before the horse. We've reversed the biblical order in our culture and placed "feelings" ahead of "committed knowledge." Is there romance in Scripture? Most certainly! Just read the Song of Solomon if you want to see romance. I almost blush as I read how that couple loved and interacted with each other. In the Song of Solomon you can see the progression: The Betrothal (1:2-3:5), the Wedding (3:6-5:1), the Life of Love (5:2-8:14).

In our culture we are taught to marry the one you love. However, nowhere in Scripture do we ever find this idea encouraged or articulated. Instead, Scripture teaches us to **love the one you marry**. If we can grasp this fact and see relationships the way the Bible sees them, then it will change how we teach and train about love and commitment versus love and feelings.

PARENTS: ARE WE AWAKENING LOVE TOO SOON?

As a parent I feel I need to admit something to you. I am more influenced than I care to admit by others. I believe as parents one of the greatest obstacles in implementing these principles is staring us in the mirror. Could it be that we, the parents, are just too afraid to implement these Scriptural principles? Could it be we are afraid of the conversations at work, or at the grocery store, or even with those in our own families, when they ask, "Why don't your kids date?" After all, peer pressure affects all ages.

Here's the problem. It's the snowball effect. What starts out as something small and cute, innocent and sweet, such as Valentine cards in the third grade and school dances in the 6th grade, often morph into sexual promiscuity by the 10th grade. We might think it's cute when Susie has a little boyfriend when she's 9 or 10. But it's not so cute when Susie is 19 or 20 and has been through numerous heartaches and emotional breakups and has the emotional scars to prove it.

The Song of Solomon repeats an interesting warning three times (2:7, 3:5, 8:4) we need to heed. Solomon tells the daughters of Jerusalem not to stir up or **awaken love too soon**. Parents, I believe we are innocently and unknowingly doing this very thing. We are allowing our children to stir up romantic desires too young. All that does is to potentially set them up to live the kind of lives we've lived or worse. They'll be apologizing for their emotional and relationship baggage one day, just like us.

Parents, this is such a critical issue. If we open the door to being romantic **prior** to a commitment, we will continue to allow our young people to be vulnerable to all the potential hurt and pain experienced in multiple breakups. I don't think this is what any of us want. I believe you want what's best for your children. You want to give them nutritious food and a good home. You want to give them a quality education and even a nice vacation. You will get them to their practices on time and prepared. You will make sure they have the right kind of cleats and the right kind of dance shoes and the right kind of musical instruments. I'm with you! We will go out of our way to make sure our children are prepared for school and prepared athletically, but what about emotionally and spiritually?

Why are we so intentionless and purposeless when it comes to desiring wholeness for our children's hearts? Can't we see that we are often awakening love too soon? When will we stop being so accepting of the broken hearts and the emotional damage (not to mention the physical) with multiple relationships throughout our children's youth? Maybe we don't know and have never really studied what the Scripture says. Maybe we are afraid of our peers or even our children and we're allowing ourselves to rationalize: "Well, I got through it. They will too. They'll be okay."

Do you really want to take that chance? I'll ask again, if you had it to do over again, wouldn't you have saved yourself for your spouse? Wouldn't you have desired **only** one relationship? I know

I'd live differently. I'd have saved myself for Pam and only Pam. Why shouldn't we want the same for our children?

Maybe we just need some courage. I've learned courage is something that wells up inside a person to the degree that person believes in the mission. Do we believe and value the mission of raising our children to be morally pure? Our sacrifice will be in direct proportion to how much we value the mission and that sacrifice will require courage. I believe in my children and the mission of protecting their hearts and teaching them to trust in the sovereignty of God and His timing for their future spouse. I desperately and sincerely want better for them than running into a former girlfriend in a grocery store and awkwardly trying to explain who the person is **that's not their mother**.

Oh, I know what I'm describing is the way less traveled, but isn't that what Jesus teaches? Isn't it the **narrow way** that leads to life and the broad way that leads to destruction? The Bible says we are to be a peculiar people. The question is: Do we have the courage to be peculiar? We teach our kids not to succumb to peer pressure. I pray we won't either. I pray we won't awaken love in our children too soon.

THE ROLE OF FATHERS

Perhaps you see that heading and are thinking, "He's just talked about parents, why is he not moving on at this point? Why is he bringing up fathers?" Well, I'm glad you asked. Dad, quite simply the Bible tells us we are to be the spiritual leader in our home. Furthermore, the Bible admonishes clearly in Ephesians 6:4: "Fathers, do not provoke your children to anger, but bring them up in the discipline and instruction of the Lord."

Dad, we have to lead in the spiritual teaching and training of our children. I wrote an entire chapter about this fact in my book, *Rite of Passage for the Home and Church: Raising Christ-Centered Young Adults*. As fathers, we have a responsibility to get our children to the wedding altar pure. Dad, if you have a daughter, please

19

realize you will one day "give her away" by placing her hand into the hand of the young man who will then assume the role of being her protective provider and spiritual leader. Up to and until that time occurs, it's your job to be her protector, provider, and spiritual leader. Remember in Genesis 2:22, it was God who brought Eve to Adam:

> And the rib that the **Lord God** had taken from the man he made into a woman and **brought her** to the man. (My emphasis added.)

God, the Father brought Eve to Adam. She was pure and chaste. That's our job, men! We are to deliver our children to the wedding altar pure and holy. But is that happening today?

There are some young "men" out there who are just pretending to be men, because they're still acting like "boys." These young "men" pull into the driveway in a car in which they didn't buy the gas nor pay for the insurance. And yet, they expect you to turn your daughter over to them for the next four to five hours … no strings attached. If this young "man" doesn't have a job and he can't afford to pay for the insurance and he's not expressed his intentions, then Dad, what are you doing allowing him to take your daughter anywhere? You are potentially **giving her away** to a young man who might crush her heart.

Let me phrase the discussion this way. Dad, would you give him the keys to your antique car and let him drive it away, no questions asked? I know that answer. Absolutely not! So then why do we so readily and easily give him our daughter? Shouldn't we know his intentions? Shouldn't we require him to sit down and declare his intentions and the purpose of the relationship? I am not saying our daughters are not smart enough to protect themselves, but it is our job to make sure they are protected.

I'm the father of three daughters and one son and it's my job to train my children to be pure and righteous. It's my job to encourage and inspire my children to seek the Lord and desire to arrive to their wedding day holy as virgins. To desire anything less is not to desire God's best. Thus, we should be having conversations and discussions with our children regularly about God's desire for them and their future mates. Dad, I would encourage you to fast and pray for your children and their future spouses. I do this one day per week and have been for years. Why? Because my kids are worth it and I know yours are too!

A Word to the Young Ladies

Ladies, I must tell you I've sought insight from my wife regarding what I'm going to share here. You are inundated with thoughts and ideas about how to find Mr. Right. You are influenced by magazines, movies (featuring "love at first sight" and "knights in shining armor"), music, romance novels, social media posts, tweets, etc. You are often made to feel you are not beautiful or desired if you don't have a boyfriend. It's easy to become frustrated and impatient, but please **do not be so hasty to give your heart away until you know what a young man plans to do with it**.

It's been my experience there are some young ladies who will quickly say, "I don't date." But, in their hearts, they would jump at the chance if an opportunity presented itself. Some girls are in love with the **idea** of being in love. It is easy to be in love with the idea of marriage. But, life is not a remake of *Romeo and Juliet*. Ladies, there is no Mr. Perfect, or Romeo out there. Marriage is not a Shakespeare play. No, I'm not saying to lower your expectations for what your potential mate should be. But often we set the standard based on the wrong things like Hollywood movies or sappy love songs. Those things are not **real** life. Do not become frustrated in waiting on God's timing so that you **settle** or you will likely end up miserable. It's okay to just be in love with serving God until He brings that young man into your life. After all, we are told to love the Lord our God with all of our soul, mind, and strength. Is He enough for you right now?

I recently heard a young lady say, "What can I gain from falling in love with a flawed, imperfect human man, when I can't even love my perfect, loving God first?" If you have the desire to marry but not the opportunity, be content and trust God. We know **coveting** is a sin. Too many ladies have a mentality to have a "ring by spring" and they end up spending their season of single life longing for marriage and then spend their married life longing to be single again. Be content and trust God no matter your circumstances. It's so easy to become blinded and self-absorbed in dissatisfaction with our current state of affairs. Yet, we must trust the hand of God. Can you become satisfied and patient with God as he orchestrates your life? Trust Him! Don't become sad or bitter. Satan wants that for your life. Don't give up on love, just understand God's timing is perfect and His love for you is perfect and His desires for you are perfect.

A WORD TO THE YOUNG MEN

Guys, please don't ask a young lady for her heart until you are ready, willing, able and fully intend to keep her heart. Remember the discussion about the biblical principle of the bride's price? In order for a young man to rightly pursue a young lady, he must be able to show he can and is willing to pay the bride's price. This means that he will follow the mandate of Genesis 2 and he will leave his father and mother and be joined to his wife and provide a way of life for her. Otherwise, he's trying to buy something he can't afford. So, young men, you have no business pursuing a young lady's heart if you can't provide for her. If your dad is still paying for the gas and insurance on your car, then scripturally speaking, you are not qualified or capable to pursue a young lady's heart. Prepare yourself now and be willing to give yourself up for your bride, even now.

The Bible has a very powerful exhortation for us regarding our duty to our wives in Ephesians 5:25: "Husbands, love your wives, as Christ loved the church and gave himself up for her."

You might be thinking, "Wait a minute. I'm just 14-years-old." Well, I want to give you a vision of seeing your future bride. Picture her in your mind. Did you know your future bride is on this earth right now and God can see her? He knows her. She's living, walking, talking and breathing just like you. Can I ask you a couple of questions? Is God's choice for you worth waiting for? Is God's choice for you worth **giving yourself up for her** even now? Ephesians 5:25 can give you a vision for the future that will drive you to surrender and sacrifice all other potential relationships and simply wait for God to bring this young lady into your life. This means you are willing to forsake all others even now. We'll often say those words in our wedding vows, "forsaking all others, keeping only unto you ..." But, will we do that now? Will we forsake all others now? Why wait to forsake all others until you put on the ring? Why not forsake all the potential relationship baggage instead? You could make that decision right now to give yourself up for her. Grab that vision! She's worth it!

So How Do We Do This?

We've covered a lot of ground and it's now time to begin to boil this thing down. Maybe you are like me and you are a "bottom line" kind of person and you are ready to get to the bottom line: **Exactly how to do this?** Well, let's all be reminded that I can't give you five easy steps (like the recipe for baking a cake). There is no cookie-cutter formula and I can't point to a specific passage of Scripture and say, "Do it like that!" Yet, I do believe we can take what we've seen thus far and begin to provide some points of admonition.

#1 Looking For a Name?

Surely by now you have noticed I've not attempted to name what I've been describing to you in this book? I haven't called it "Dating with Purpose," or "Dating Friendships" or "Neighbor Relationships," "Courtship," or "Covenant Relationship." While all of those terms have meaning in their own right, I don't want to give a name or title to this process other than what the Bible calls it: **betrothal**. You see, it matters not so much what you **call** this process, it matters more that you seek the Father in implementing His Word in your life. We are to be more than just hearers of the Word. We are to be **doers** of the Word.

#2 Preparation

Often when we think about relationships, we think mostly about the end result. Seldom do we consider the preparation involved so we might arrive successfully at the intended conclusion. It's so easy to become enamored by good looks, athletic prowess, intelligence or popularity when considering someone to pursue. But preparation, character and purity should be considered first. We can become so engrossed in finding the right life partner that we forget we need to become the right life partner, trusting God to orchestrate the "who" and "when." In short, we need to prepare.

Part of that preparation is purposing to remain pure, taking proper advantage of your singleness and building wholesome relationships that cause one to treat younger men as **brothers** and younger women as **sisters**. Too often that's not the case in our culture. It seems the goal is to find the handsome hunk or the gorgeous gal. Let's not be superficial. For those of us who are married, we know marriage is about more than appearance and physical attraction. God told the prophet Samuel not to look on the outward appearance, but at the heart.

So what should you be thinking about in regard to a mate? Here are some considerations:

> » What's on the inside?
> » What kind of personality do they have?
> » What kind of personal discipline do they have?
> » Can they get along with others?
> » Do they have a work ethic?
> » How about a sense of humor?
> » How do they handle stress?
> » Can they handle money?

- » How do they relate to God?
- » Is there a righteousness and purity about their demeanor?
- » Will they draw you closer to God or pull you away?
- » How do they talk, dress, act?
- » How do they handle pressure?
- » What's their attitude toward their parents?
- » How do they speak to and treat their parents?
- » How do they treat their siblings and other children?
- » Do they love Jesus?
- » The Bible?
- » The church?

These are the things that really matter. Now go back and read the list again and ask yourself if you embody those characteristics.

Let's place emphasis and focus on the process of preparation and in becoming the person God wants us to be and leave the timing to God. He knows exactly (at this very moment) who your mate, or your child's mate is to be. We don't have to help the Creator of the universe do His work. He's very capable. Trust Him and trust His sovereign timing. Young person, use this time in your life to prepare yourself to become the mate that your future spouse is praying for. If you are single right now, don't waste this **season** of your life by coveting someone else's life. Your singleness is only temporary (even though God does call some to remain single, like the Apostle Paul). Just remember, you've not failed if you don't get married or if you aren't married by a certain time. Don't pine away. Surrender your will to the Lord, serve Him and trust Him to take care of the rest.

#3 Don't Worry about What Everyone Else is Doing

I am convinced one of our biggest issues in deciding how we are going to live our lives is simply making up our minds not to be influenced by the culture. In other words, it doesn't matter what everyone else is doing. I know every TV show has boyfriends and girlfriends. I know most of the people you know are going to continue to date. I know social media is going to continue to drive the culture. But, that shouldn't surprise us. Art and entertainment are simply reflections of our society.

We've all been conditioned to **fall in love**. But, **love is sacrifice, not a Hollywood movie ending**. We've got to stop allowing ourselves and our children to be conditioned by the culture. Your son or daughter will be expected to pair up with other 11 year-olds at the middle school dance. (By the way, that's mind-blowing to me. What's next … first grade dances? How young will they go?) Just realizing how we've been conditioned by the culture is half the battle.

The Bible says, "Whoever walks with the wise, becomes wise, but the companion of fools will suffer harm" (Prov. 13:20). Parents, the peers your teen hangs around will have a huge impact on them. Let's be honest. Your teen and mine can't be immersed in a culture of friends who aren't living for God and not have negative influence rub off on them. Almost by osmosis … the ways of the world will seep into them. You can count on that. So, I encourage you to know your children's friends and know them well, for it is likely they will have a tremendous impact on whether or not your teen will embrace the principles in this book.

#4 Observe, Observe, Observe

It is good to observe someone's life in **real life** situations in group settings. Remember dating is artificial and it often creates a façade. So, look for opportunities to observe someone you might consider God's man or woman for you at your church or working on a team mission trip. Being **alone** with someone you care about is very dangerous. All too often the emotions begin to do the thinking.

So consider having younger siblings present if you are going to move the relationship outside of the home or church group setting. We did this with our daughter Katy prior to her marriage.

Kandace, who is almost four years younger, tagged along with Katy and Josh from time to time. They both knew being alone with no one around could potentially end up in physical compromise. 1 Thessalonians 4:1-8 speaks clearly about self-control and God's will that we abstain from sexual activity. Group settings provide accountability and protection, and help to maintain purity and wholesomeness for a couple.

#5 Begin Young

Those of you reading this who have young children, begin now. Begin when your children are young discussing what the Bible has to say about relationships. Point out the fact God knows exactly who it is He wants them to marry. Raise the bar. Encourage them to go for the gold medal, if you will. Don't settle. **Our children will always rise to the level of our expectations.**

It's obviously much easier for a child to accept these principles than it is for a teenager. It's not impossible for a teenager to adopt these principles to live by, but it's much harder than for the young person under the age of 12. Parents, realize you have a wonderful opportunity to begin shaping the expectations of your child. As the old saying goes, "Don't wait until they've already put the boat in the water before you tell them it's too soon to go sailing."

You see, if we truly believe God is all-powerful and His word is the authority in our lives, then we will teach our children to trust Him in all things at a young age. We will teach our children to be courageous enough to be **peculiar** as the Bible teaches. In fact, if you will build this kind of thinking into their minds, you will rejoice with them as they realize the pressure is off and they can simply spend their teenage years growing spiritually without the pressure of a relationship which only adds to the many demands they already have as young adults.

One of the best ways to impart truth to our children is by simply talking to them. Keep them talking. Bed time particularly seems to be an important time in the lives of children. They seem to be most open and willing to talk. Ultimately, they desire you, Mom and Dad. After all, rules without a relationship usually lead to some form of rebellion. I know, for me, I'm often really tired at night after long days, but that's when my children like to talk. So we do. We talk about life. We talk about their day. We talk about the hopes and dreams their mom and I have for their future. It's during those times that my wife and I continue to plant the seeds of Scripture in the fertile soil of their young minds. God's word, once it takes root, will bear fruit by forging the character in their young lives that will be able to stand strong and bear the ridicule and pressure of the peer-driven teen years.

KATY AND JOSH

You've now read the majority of this book and you might be thinking, "Okay, all this sounds good, but will it work?" The answer is: yes, indeed it can. It's God's plan after all. God's word will not return void. These aren't man-made theories. These are principles gleaned from the timeless Scriptures. And yes, I have a real life example for you. Here it is:

That's my daughter, Katy and my son-in-law, Josh Isaacs. They were married on November 10, 2012. Katy never dated. Josh did and he'll tell you if he had it to do over again, he would have waited for Katy.

Katy never dated. She never got her heart tied up and tangled up with another guy. In fact, her first kiss was given to Josh on their wedding day. Some have asked me, "How did you make Katy do this?" Truly, Pam and I didn't make her do anything. The truth is: you can't really **make** a child choose this path. At some point they have to **own their own faith and convictions.** Katy chose to walk down this road with road signs along the way that said: **Commitment, Parent Involvement,** and **Purposeful Intentionality**, guided by God and His word.

I want you to know this lifestyle can be lived and this can be done. Now, please understand, your story will not be like Katy's story. No two stories are exactly alike. The same is true with our salvation. Your story is not like my story. But, we've arrived at the same destination. Katy decided when she was a little girl she wanted to save all of her heart and all of her kisses for her future husband. Like an Olympian, she chose to go for gold! It wasn't easy. It was a tough pull. But she took the principles of Scripture we taught her and embodied them and received them into her heart and spirit.

I was once told by a man, "You're lying. It's impossible! She had to have kissed a guy!" But that's simply not true. She chose to never put herself into that situation. We had taught her from the time she was a little girl about what happens to the heart and emotions once a couple becomes close emotionally. But Katy also knew she needed to surround herself with friends who were like-minded. She recognized if all her friends were dating, the peer pressure would likely become too much. This is true for any of us. We tend to become like the people we hang out with the most. But I don't want to tell you any more about Katy's journey, because she can tell you herself. She's written a book entitled, *The Unbroken Road*. Information on how you can obtain it is located at the end of this book.

Honestly, I chose to show you Katy and Josh's picture above because I know a picture can speak a thousand words. I wanted to inspire you. That's ultimately what I've been trying to do throughout this entire book. It's been said, "Nothing great is accomplished without inspiration."

CONCLUSION

In this book, I've tried to describe to you what the Bible says about premarital relationships and show you the parallels of how God describes His relationship with His Son and His church. If you want a bottom line though, it will be impossible for me to give you one. I've tried to show you what God has designed for two people of the opposite sex to do to get to know each other, under the protection of a loving family, who will help guard the couple against impurity until marriage.

Some will say: "But I'm afraid I won't have the discipline, focus, or time to make this a reality in the lives of my children." Some might say, "But I want details! I need details! How am I supposed to navigate these waters without more information?" Well, I'll summarize these questions by saying this to you one last time: **If you were looking for a detailed, formulaic, step-by-step process for handling premarital relationships, you won't get that**

from me. Why? Because I'm convinced God wants us to look to Him through this process and for all things in life. He wants us to depend on Him. He wants us to seek Him in prayer and rest in Him. Isn't that the Christian life in a nutshell: "Walking by faith and not by sight" (2 Cor. 5:7).

My goals here were to bring you encouragement, inspiration and hope as you consider what the Bible teaches about premarital relationships. My heartfelt prayer is this book will impact your life and the lives of your children by potentially saving them from the "mini-divorces" so common even in Christendom today. I pray the next generation of children will not have the emotional, **relationship baggage** many of us have had to deal with in our adult lives.

I believe the focus of all life should be Jesus Christ and our desire should be to bring Him glory. He offers salvation to all who will repent of their sins and call on His name and for those who have received this great gift, much is required. We're called to take the message of His good news to the world. It's called the Great Commission (Matt. 28:19-20).

I see marriage as a crucible that refines us for eternity. God has used my marriage to my lovely bride to help me be a better servant for Christ. We have leveraged our relationship together for our Lord and Master, King Jesus. Pam and I understand the finish line in this life is not marriage; it is heaven! Let's teach this lifestyle to our children today. It's not too late to start. It's not how you start; it's how you finish. In Christ, we can make up for lost time.

Jesus is coming again to gather His bride, the Church, to Himself. He'll take us to the prepared place (heaven), where a wedding will commence, followed by a grand reception. Marriage is part of God's divine plan to make us holy and that won't necessarily always make us happy. But it's part of the sanctifying process to prepare us for the ultimate marriage in heaven. To the young person reading this book I conclude with these words: I pray that you will one day find as much joy in marriage as I have and you will remember the ultimate goal in all of life is glorifying God through his Son, the Lord Jesus Christ.

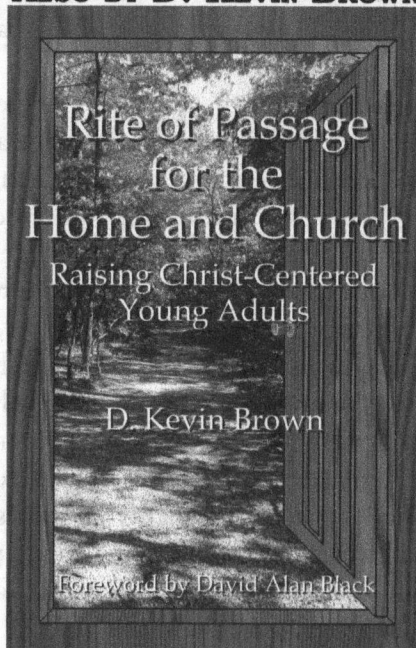

THE TOPICAL LINE DRIVES SERIES

(All volumes are $4.99 print and $0.99 in ebook formats)

Currently Available

The Authorship of Hebrews: The Case for Paul	David Alan Black
What Protestants Need to Know about Roman Catholics	Robert LaRochelle
Forgiveness: Finding Freedom from Your Past	Harvey Brown, Jr.
Holistic Spirituality:	
Life-Giving Wisdom from the Letter of James	Bruce G. Epperly
Process Theology: Embracing Adventure with God	Bruce G. Epperly
To Date or Not to Date: What the Bible Teaches about	
Premarital Relationships	D. Kevin Brown

Forthcoming:

God the Creator	Henry E. Neufeld
What Roman Catholics Need to Know about Protestants	Robert LaRochelle
The Authority of Scripture in a Postmodern Age:	
Some Help from Karl Barth	Robert D. Cornwall
The Eucharist: Encounters with Jesus at the Table	Robert D. Cornwall

MORE FROM ENERGION PUBLICATIONS

Except for Fornication (Areopagus)	H. VanDyke Parunak	$9.99
Life as Pilgrimage	David Moffett-Moore	14.99
From Inspiration to Understanding	Edward W. H. Vick	$24.99
My Life Story	Becky Lynn Black	$14.99
The Jesus Paradigm	David Alan Black	$17.99
The Sacred Journey	Chris Surber	$11.99
When People Speak for God	Henry Neufeld	$17.99

Generous Quantity Discounts Available
Dealer Inquiries Welcome
Energion Publications — P.O. Box 841
Gonzalez, FL 32560
Website: http://energion.com
Phone: (850) 525-3916